Living in Space

Written by Hannah Reed

Flying Start
to Literacy®

Contents

Chapter 1
The International Space Station

The International Space Station is a place where people can live in space for months at a time. It was built in 1998 by people from 15 countries.

The people who live in the International Space Station are called astronauts. They live and work on the space station. Astronauts learn more about what it is like in space and how living in space affects living things.

Hundreds of people on Earth work to keep the International Space Station flying safely in space.

Getting there

Astronauts fly to the International Space Station in space shuttles.

Everything that the astronauts will need while they live in space is brought by the shuttles to the space station. This includes food, water, clothing and science equipment.

When the shuttle goes back to Earth it takes away all the rubbish from the space station.

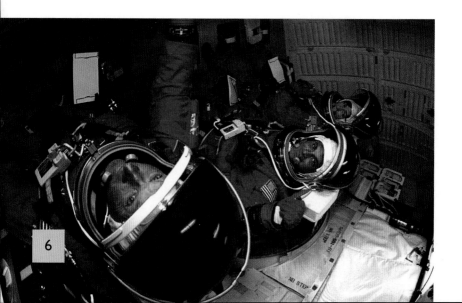

Chapter 2
Living in space

Living in space is difficult. There is no air or water. It is cold and dark and people cannot survive in space without the protection of the space station.

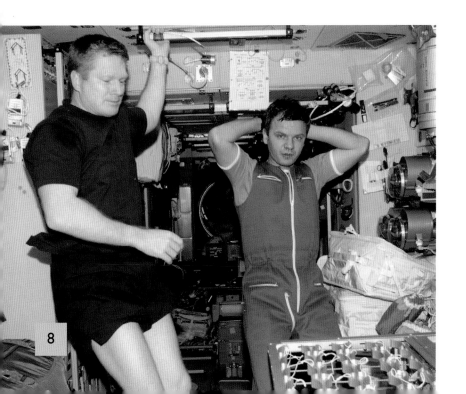

In space there is much less gravity than on Earth. When you drop something on Earth it falls towards the ground. This is because of gravity.

In space the gravity is so weak that things float around as if they have no weight. The gravity in space is called microgravity.

The space station is set up so that astronauts can survive in space.

Air is pumped through the space station. It is cleaned and recycled all the time so that it is safe for the astronauts to breathe.

The space station has heating and lighting so that the astronauts stay warm and can see around them. There are kitchens, bathrooms and places for the astronauts to sleep.

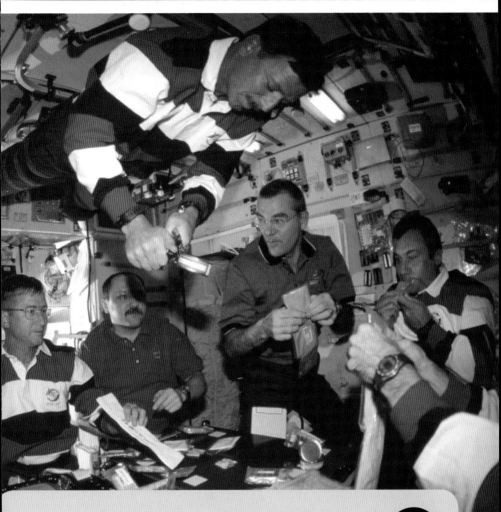

People from around the world work together to run the International Space Station. Astronauts from the USA, Russia, Canada, Japan and the European Space Agency work there.

Space food

Astronauts living in the space station eat some of the same food that you or I would eat, but some of it is very different.

They eat fresh fruit and vegetables, dried food, and drinks such as long-life milk and juice. Some foods, such as soup, come in packages that can be heated in microwave ovens.

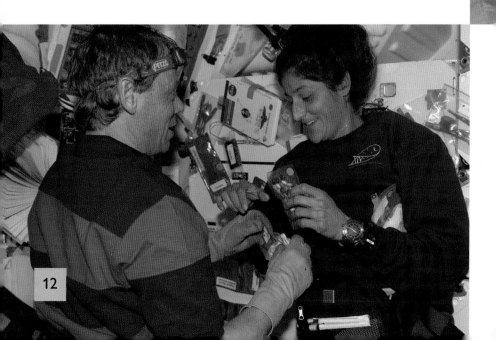

Astronauts don't eat foods with crumbs
such as toast. This is because in the
space station the crumbs float around and
can cause problems if they get into people's
eyes or into the computer keyboards. Some
foods are coated in a jelly to stop them
making crumbs.

Water in space

All of the water on the space station needs to be used carefully because only a limited amount of water can be taken there.

On the space station, no water is wasted and it needs to be recycled. To do this, as much water as possible is collected, cleaned and used over and over again.

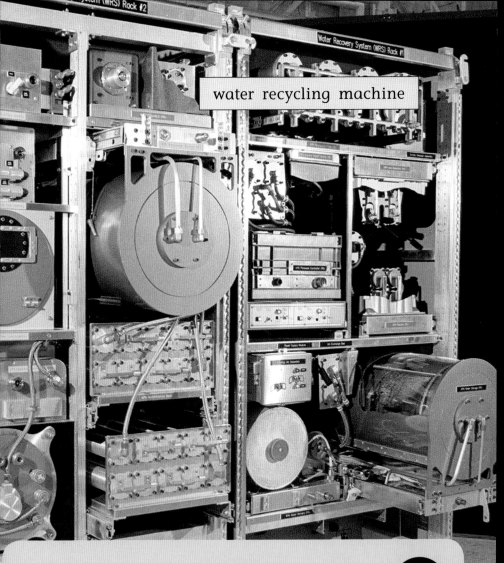

water recycling machine

Space fact

The water that is cleaned and recycled comes from all parts of the space station including the bathrooms.

Sleeping in space

When astronauts sleep in space they have to stop themselves from floating around and bumping into things. They sleep in sleeping bags and strap themselves onto pods or seats to sleep.

Astronauts often wear a sleeping mask over their eyes when they sleep. This is because as the space station moves through space, the sun comes up every 90 minutes.

Space fact

Space station sleeping cabins have windows that look out into space.

Chapter 3
Working in space

Astronauts do experiments and look after the space station. The experiments are often about how things work in space.

In one experiment, astronauts planted corn seeds. The roots of the corn plants did not grow straight down. Instead they grew in many different directions.

Astronauts can see the Earth from the space station. They collect photographs of the Earth. These photographs show how the Earth looks different after an earthquake or when a volcano erupts.

Building in space

Astronauts add new parts to the space station to make it bigger. The new sections for the space station are built on Earth and then loaded into a space shuttle. The shuttle then takes them to the space station.

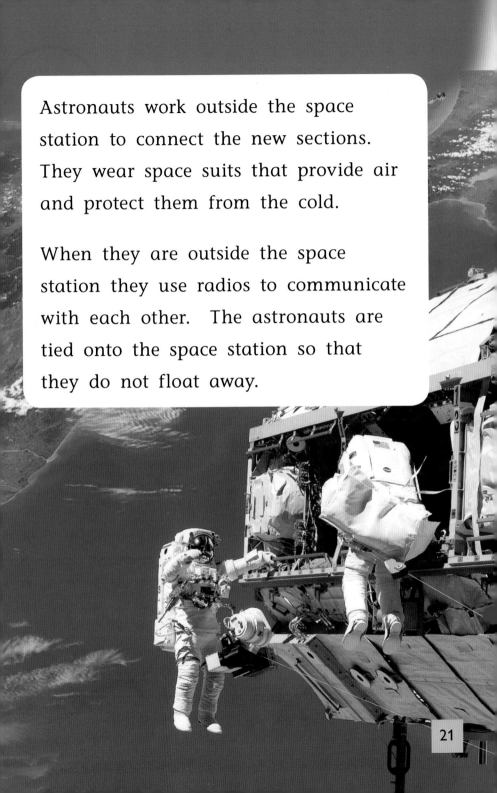

Astronauts work outside the space station to connect the new sections. They wear space suits that provide air and protect them from the cold.

When they are outside the space station they use radios to communicate with each other. The astronauts are tied onto the space station so that they do not float away.

Chapter 4
The future

In the future many people might live in space. They might be able to grow food and use water so that it will not have to be brought from Earth.

Learning to live in space might make it
possible for people to travel further and
further into space to explore places that
no one has been to before.

Glossary

astronaut a person trained to travel or work in space

gravity the force that causes objects to pull towards each other

recycled to process something so that it can be used again

space the place where the solar system, stars and galaxies exist

space shuttle a space craft that takes astronauts into space and returns them to Earth

survive to stay alive